LA VIE- A MATTER OF CHOICES

"EVERYTHING THAT HAPPENS TO YOU MATTERS"

SHREENMAY KANUNGO

SOLEMNLY DEDICATED/DEVOTED TO- Mrs.
DIPTIMAYI KANUNGO, Mr. SASANKA SEKHAR
KANUNGO

೮೩

_"Without the inspiration, drive, and support that you have
given me, I might not be the person I am today."_

Contents

FOREWORD

<u>your story is unique, And so different... not WORTHY of comparison!</u>
If not now, when? There are some *livres* you pick out because you know they'll be tear- jerkers, and you're not opposed to a good cry. Then there are the *livres* that sucker- punch you with a tragic plot twist that leaves you dribbling tears and snot onto the pages.
The very first reads have the ability to elicit full range of emotions, even if that entails a little heartbreak

∛

"La vie- A Matter of Choices"- Life is about choices. Some we regret, some we're proud of. Some will haunt us forever. The message: We are what we chose to be.
La vie- A Matter of Choices- contains various ascpects of life, and how to respect them, how to struggle to get sucess or come out of a difficult situation. It also shows how to help others in times of need.
The book-
will taught the art of war of intelligibility,
And providence of gesticulation...
I am as a matter of fact enormously
beholden, bounden to it.....
No agitation-
No thunderbolt-
No shilly-shallying-
No indecision, hesitation-

ACKNOWLEDGEMENTS

Foremost, I would like to express my sincere gratitutude to my advisor- Dr. Sasanka Sekhar Kanungo, for the continuous support, for his patience, motivation, and immense knowledge. His guidance helped me in all the time of writing. I could notr have imagined having a better advisor and mentor for my book- "La vie- A Matter of Choices".

Besides my advisor, I would like to thank the rest of my manuscript proof reading committe ; *SACHIN VAISHNAV, DIVYA MARCHANDINI, JPC MISRA, JYOTI RANJAN SAHU* .

The members/well-wishers/teachers/principals- of my school- LOYOLA SCHOOL, BHUBANESWAR deserve to be thanked for they have inspired me too redeem my long cherished dream.

my happiness and ceaseless effort will be multiplied if this book serves the requirements of the readers the best.

PROLOGUE

'Hello , This is Stephen a storyteller, like l would when l will become a man. And today l will share you some stories l have heard from my grandma. So, let's start'

**Why Stephen?** What Hawking overcame, and what he went on to accomplish is beyond extraordinary and completely inspiring. His refusal to give up his intellectual pursuits in spite of his condition, is the personification of persistence.

Now the first story is a sort of adventurous and I hope you all like it so let's start.

I

THE JOURNEY OF FANTASY: SECRET REALM

The society manager was angry at gangsters: Raj, Shina, Riya and Rahul. They always flout his rules and tell him a grouch. So today he got hold of them but still they were able to ran away. While running, they decided to go to Raj's house as their parents were there. After running, they were thirsty, suddenly Grandma Imana arrived, she had bought drinks for them, all of four kids were happy and then while drinking Grandma asked 'Children do you want to go on a trip?'

'Yes' all of them shouted.

'So we will go to my friend's farmhouse at Parwathpur ' said Grandma.

All of them agreed and then packed the bags for the journey

The journey was beautiful and the place was amazing. All the four met Mrs. Anuradha, whose farmhouse they went. She was a charming woman who was also hospitiable Mrs. Anuradha introduced Radhika to all of them. Radhika was an amiable and caring girl. All of them became friends very soon and Radhika told them a secret. She said with tears 'My mother had died 3 years ago and my father remarried but seeing stepmother's activities he committed suicide and now my stepmother is ill-treating my grandfather, grandmother and me'. Everyone consoled her but they could do nothing.

The morning of 21st June (the day when anything magical can happen) was beautiful. Everything was going just fine when a note came from Grandma Amana. It stated, 'Children, come down to basement, I will show you, something'. All of them went to the basement but suddenly the door closed. All of them got frightened and then someone spoke 'You all will pay the price for coming here'. It was Radhika's stepmother. All of them shouted for help but all in vain. They started sobbing when suddenly Shina spotted something, it was a circular object with fantasian world stated on it. Raj saw a button and pressed it. All of them were drawn into the circular object.

On opening their eyes, they found themselves in a very stinky and dirty place. Then something from the bushes spoke 'Who are you all and what are you doing here?'. It was a big stinky ogre. Before saying anything they were taken to the castle where the king announced they should be thrown into the jail. After being thrown away, they again started sobbing and prayed God, suddenly a woman with a stick dressed blue came. She said that she would help but all of them were scared. She said that they didn't need to be scared and they could trust her. Her warmness made them feel that she was a good woman and therefore they followed her. They all started running while running Shina said Radhika that she could join the gangsters after this but suddenly a bomb fell right in front of them. All of them fell in different regions, still the gangsters were able to come out of the circular object, then suddenly Shina asked 'Where is Radhika?'

Where was Radhika, what would all of them do next. To find the answer read the next part.

II
JOURNEY OF FANTASY: FINAL FIGHT

Suddenly Shina asked 'where is Radhika?' Everyone's face turned pale then Raj said 'We have left her in the fantasian world'. All of them decided to return to the Fantasian world to save Radhika. They pressed the button and then they were drawn inside the object. The place was same but now they had a task to complete, they put themselves in the luggage of the ogres and went inside the castle. After coming out they went to the prison. They saw Radhika and the lady in blue. All of them (the gangsters) helped Radhika and the lady in blue to come out and then they hugged each other. All were happy and started running to the exit but suddenly someone threw a sword which pierced through the lady in blue, she fell to the ground. It was king of ogres. He shouted 'Now you all will be dead'.He threw a smog bomb which made Everyone tired that they fell down, now it was only God who could save them. After sometime, with a blurry vision Raj could see many fairies fighting with the ogres but he was so tired that he slept , when they woke up , they were in the the storeroom, the circular object was not there. 'It was a dream' said Shina then they went to their parents and grandparents, they told about what had Radhika's stepmother done , she was put behind the bars and after that everyone lived happily ever after.

THE REAL SECRET IS IT WAS NOT A DREAM BUT A TRUTH

'Ok so the story is over'

'Ting tong bell'

'Someone came let me see'

'Oh it's grandma' said Stephen

'Hello , you are telling stories and you didn't invite me'

'ok live it, now you sit 1 will tell some stories' said Grandma

'Ok granny' said Stephen

Now the story is about a boy who was very courageous. This story is my favourite and 1 hope its your too.

III

ALAIN RICHARDS: A BOY FROM SMILEVILLE

The sun was shining brightly in the crystal clear sky. Winds were blowing with the taste of yesterday's rain in them. Cows were grazing in the field and little Alain was playing with his dog, Trumpet. The morning was the best time to enjoy.

'Trumpet', called Alain with a smile on his face, 'Do you know Mommy and Daddy are going to the market today to sell the crops and Daddy has told he would bring a toy for me' said Alain happily.

'Alain, come here' called Mrs Richards.

'Mom, are you not going to the market?' asked Alain.

'No child, the market is closed for us' said Mrs. Richards in a downhearted tone.

'But Why?' asked Alain.

'Because of the lady' said Mrs. Richards.

'Who is the lady?' asked Alain in an antagonized tone.

Mrs Richards started explaining 'The name of our town is smileville but in reality the town is covered with the clouds of .... and sorrow. The reason is Ageuliata Martin, queen of wickedness. She is though not the mayor of our town but has more power than the chief minister of our state. The mayors, high post officers as well as the chief ministers are all a kind of servants to her. She has killed 4000 people and has set 100 villages on fire. If someone doesnot surrenders her, she kills everyone of their family.'

'She is scary' said Alain

'Ys, but 3 years ago she was a good woman after her husband's death she changed' said Mrs. Richards and went away.

Alain was dejected, he went to the fields and sat on a big rock.

Suddenly a girl spoke 'Hii, why are you sad?'

Alain turned and said 'Who are you and why should I tell you?'

'Ok don't tell, By the way my name is Sophia' said the girl.

'Oh great, what a name you have but mine is better. My name is Alain Richards' said Alain.

They played for sometime and then went to their homes.

Days went by and one day Mr. Richards came home in a frustrated mood.

'I am tired of this new mayor, what does the think about him, is he a king' said Richards in a vexatious tone.

'What happened?' asked Mrs Richards.

'That mayor has declared that the southern side of the town won't sell their crops' said Mr. Richards.

' This is not good , you should file a complaint against the mayor in the police station', said Mrs Richards

'Yes, I will' saying this Mr. Richards went to thepolice station

Alain was watching this, he was upset that their crops are not going to be sold in the market. He went to the fields and sat on the giant rock.

'Alain, are you ok?' asked Sophia.

'Ya a kind of not, the new mayor is just insane, he thinks he can do whatever he wants, he is very bad.' Said Alain, 'But father has gone to file a complaint against him' said Alain, with a smile on his face.

Sophia's face turned pale and she ran to her house.

Alain did not understand anything and asked 'Why are running?'

With a worried face, she said 'Your father should not file a case against the mayor'.

Saying this she went away.

Alain thought it was a joke so he didn't take it seriously and then he came home, ate dinner and went to sleep.

Next morning, Mr and Mrs Richards went to the hospital as Mrs. Richards was pregnant. They bid Alain goodbye and went to the hospital. Alain was very happy that he was going to have a brother or a sister.

When Mr. and Mrs. Richards came back, Alain was elated, he ran to see the baby, it was so cute. Alain had a sister now. They named her Sylvie Richards. Everything was going the best but happiness does not last forever.

At night, someone banged at the door, everyone got scared, Mr. Richards opened the door. They were astonished to see Mrs. Ageuliata Martin.

'Salute Mr. Richards' said the lady.

'The lady, you are here to meet me, is something wrong?' Mr Richards asked shivering with fear.

'Ya, I have come to ask you why have you filed a complaint against the mayor, Don't you know he is my brother?' she asked.

'I am sorry I didn't know that' said Mr. Richards.

'Oh, but you have done a mistake, now pay the price' she said.

Mr. Richards closed the door, packed everything and went out through the back door with his family. They reached the railway station and were getting ready to enter into the train when a bullet shot in Mr Richards chest. He fell to the ground, lifeless. Mrs. Richards could not bear it and jumped from the train and cried keeping hands on her husband's body. Alain was bawling, he was very sad. Just then, the lady came, Mrs. Richards gave Sylvie to Alain and told –

'I will stop them, you go to the city and take care of Sylvie'.

'But Mom, I can't leave you alone' Alain said with tears.

'I say go' Mrs Richards shouted.

Alain went into the moving train and in a blink of his eye Agueliata killed his mother.

'Mom' he shouted but he could do nothing.

'Agueliata' Alain roared in anger 'you would pay the price' he said in a loud tone.

Why did Sophia's face turned pale after hearing that Alain's father has filed a case against the mayor? Why did Agueliata's behaviour changed after her husband's death? Is there a mystery about it? What is Alain's next step?

To find answers, read the next part.

IV
ALAIN RICHARDS: THE RETURN

'Good morning sir, you have an interview with Jessilina at 7 PM' said Britny, the secretary.

'Yes, I am ready, let's go'.

In the interview – Jessilina said 'good evening Europe, this is Jessilina from 'Lets Interview' today we have a special guest, the one who is admired by everyone, please meet Mr. Alain Richards.'

'Hello everyone' said the 25 aged young man Alain.

The interview lasted for an hour and then Alain came home.

It was an hectic day for Alain, he was tired, so he was going to the bedroom but his eyes got distracted from the ray of light that was coming from the storeroom. He went there, the shiny object was his childhood photos. The photos were beautiful but it reminded his childhood, the lady, his parents and the cries of his mother.

He got emotional as well as angry and decided to go to the village once again. Hecanceled all his schedules for one month and then he called his sister.

'Sylvie, we are going to Smileville' said Alain.

'Bro, I can't go, you know I am busy' Sylvie said.

'Ya, busy in parties' said Alain.

'Whatever' said Sylvie.

'Sorry little sister you are going and no objections cause you know what can I do' said Alain.

'Ok, I am in' said Sylvie with a puffed face.

The journey was beautiful and the place was the same. Alain said 'Dear sis, this is Smileville'.

'Wow, such a wonderful place but covered with evilness of Agueliata' said Sylvie.

'Ya, that's true' said Alain.

They got down from the train and went to their house. An unexpected sight was seen, their house was blazed to ashes. All their memories in the house had been demolished to nothing. Tears rolled down Alain's chicks, he was heartbroken. Sylvie tried to console him and then he said 'Now we will live in Agueliata's house.'

'But how' asked Sylvie.

'You just wait and watch' said Alain with a smile.

They went to the lady's mansion. It was an old building but with a strong foundation. There was a private pool and garden. It had a lake and flowering pots beside it on the right side and in the left side it had an aguarium with a mini zoo.

Alain and Sylvie were amazed to see such a mansion, suddenly a voice distracted them. It was of a boy.

'Alain' he said 'How are you?' asked the boy.

'Yes, my name is Alain and I am fine, but who are you?' said Alain.

'I am Louise Simon, your best friend' said Louise.

Alain quickly recognized him and hugged Louise. They started chatting with each other. But suddenly a hard voice broked the conversation. It was Agueliata's.

'What are you doing here?' asked Agueliata Martin.

'We have come here to ask if you have some job for my sister and me' said Alain.

'Ya, sure, you can be servants' said Agueliata.

'Thank you, Miss' said Alain.

'And tell Louise to come and start his work' said Agueliata with a stern face.

They all went inside and started working. Alain narrated what had happened till now to Louise. Louise was sad and told that he would help them.

Then, a woman came and said 'Hello, my name is Charlotte Martin, Agueliata Martin's daughter-in-law'.

'Hello my name is Alain, this is my sister Sylvie ' said Alain.

'You're quite cute, first let me introduce you to my family' said Charlotte Martin.

'This is my husband Arthus Martin, my sister-in-law Coralie Martin, her husband Lucas Martin and her children Jeanetta Martin and Adam Martin. This is our special maid Alietto Popplewell and this is Fatterson and Thinus Martin, Mother-in-law's body guards' said Charlotte Martin.

'Ok, but who is that girl beside the sofa?' asked Alain.

'Oh, ya, I'm sorry, she is my daughter Sophia Martin' said Charlotte Martin.

Alain's face turned pale, it was the same Sophia that he had met in the hills. She was the grand-daughter of Agueliata and therefore she knew what her grandma could do. After everyone went, Alain went and told his identity, he also told the story of his childhood to till date. She felt bad for it but she could do nothing and therefore she just consoled Alain and went away.

Then suddenly, Sylvie came and asked Alain.

'Bro, how could you let us in?' she asked.

'It was simple, I told two servants that Agueliata Madam has said they can go for a holiday by showing them fake notice. They went away and then we got their positions,' Alain whispered.

'Wow, you're getting smarter living with me' said Sylvie laughing.

Days changed to months and months changed to years. Alain's business. in the city was going well and he had also put a good impression on the family of Martin.

Then one day, as Alain was coming from the kitchen, he heard a voice. It was of Agueliata's coming from her room. Alain went to the door and stood at a side.

He heard 'God, till now you have saved me from my truth and after that also you will save me. No one should know about the old servent, or else I would be exposed.'

Alain could not understand anything, he went and asked Sophia about it. She got astonished to hear about it and told to ask her mother. They both went and Alain asked her.

'Mam, who was the servant before Alietto?'

She said 'her name was Truenta, actually it was given by Mother-in-law but her actual name started with A'.

'Where did she live Mom?' asked Sophia.

'She lived in Zebosville' said Mrs. Martin.

'Due to her, Mother-in-law's behaviour changed, she started killing people, stopped Jeanetta and Sophia's schooling, changed Carolie's surname and had not allowed me to go to my home since 20 years' said Mrs.

Martin sobbing.

They consoled her and then after dinner started discussing about today's happenings. Alain, Sophia, Louise and Sylvie came and decided at the last of the conversation that they would visit Zebosville to find the real truth of Grandma.

At that time Agueliata had gone to visit the chief minister, so they had two days between which they could go to Zebosville, find the truth and came back. Nobody would guess that they are going to Zebosville.

They bid goodbye to everyone and went. The journey was a tiring one and therefore they decided to take rest at a hotel. The name of the place and the actual place are two different things. Zebosville was filled with garbage and insects. 'The cleaning department of Government never comes here and as a result this has happened' said Sophia.

They went to hotel, though old and dirty but still adjustable. They all slept for sometime and then went for their research, they searched and talked with everyone but all in vain, they found nothing. Alain was sad and then suddenly he saw an old man who had lost his stick and was searching for it. He helped him and then asked 'Grandpa, do you know Truenta Cartier'.

'Ya, she is my daughter' said grandpa.

'What' shouted Alain with surprise.

'Ya, she is my daughter, actually her name is Ataileuga Cartier but her name was changed by her mistress' said grandpa. He (Grandpa) also said 'And my daughter comes to visit me every Sunday.'

'Ok, thank you' said Alain and all them went to the hotel.

'So, the real name of Truenta is Ataileuga' said Alain.

All were discussing except Sophia, Alain went to ask her what had happened, then she said –

'You know something is strange, Truenta and Grandma both go the meet Father and Chief Minister respectively every Sunday but I was surfing the net and found out that our state's chief minster had gone to Maldives since one month, then whom is Grandma meeting to.'

Alain sat and started thinking about it and then his face was filled with nervousness and surprise.

He called everyone and said 'Guys, I understood secret of Grandma.'

Everyone was happy and asked what is it.

He said 'Ataileuga and Grandma are same.'

None believed him but then he told the reason 'Atailuega, if reversed forms Ageuliata, the name of Grandma and as Sophia 's mother had told the name starts with A.'

He also said 'She always comes to visit her father every Sunday.'

Everyone was surprised, they packed their bags and then went to Smileville.

After reaching home, they saw something they never expected, everyone was tied up and Agueliata was waiting for them.

Alain said 'Agueliata leave them or else we will tell yoursecret to everyone.'

'Oh, I am scared, boy, you think all these 23 years what am I doing. The villagers will not listen to any of you. Fatterson and Thinus capture them'.

All of them were tied up. After two days, Agueliata came and said 'Alain, today I want you to see the death of everyone, Fatterson bring him without the rope.'

Alain came out, everything was decorated and the whole town had came. Agueliata was going to give a speech but before that she came switching off the mic to Alain in the backstage.

She said 'Do you know, Alain, I think you should know why am I doing this.'

Alain switched on the other mic he had and started listening her.

'I am Ataileuga, I only killed Sophia's Grandpa and do you know I have only killed your parents, except them I have killed no one. All the rumors about me were spread by my guards. These foolish villagers are easy to fool and therefore I am on the top. The chief minsters, high-post officers aren't my servents, all these are lies. You would never understand cause you help everyone and I have also killed that old man, my father who told you all these. Now I will give a speech and then there would be a bomb blast. The bombs are under the feet of the people, if you can then save them, then save' she said and went to the stage.

When she entered the stage, the villagers ran towards her and started beating, then the police captured her. Alain came and said 'You think villagers are foolish but it is you who is foolish. You were so proud of yourself that you told everything without knowing that I had turned the mic on. Have a great time behind the bars.' Then the police took her away. Everyone was untied and the whole town was happy. Now the bomb diffusers came and the bombs were diffuse but still Alain was not happy. Sophia asked him why he wasn't happy, then he said 'If Ataileuga did not love her father then why did she went to Zebosville every Sunday?'

The four of them went to Zebosville, asked Ataileuga's house and went there.It was a cave, they went in and found an old woman. It was Grandma Ageuliata, the real grandmother of Sophia. All of them were happy and went to Smileville.

The whole town was happy to see her and then everyone started celebrating. Sylvie came asked 'Bro, how could Atailuega take the place of Ageuliata, they both have different faces?'

'My sis, didn't you understand, she had done a plastic surgery.'

'Oh, ya I understood now.'

Both of them laughed and then went to the hall. Grandma Agueliata came and declared that Sophia and Alain would marry soon and Alain would be the new mayor. Smileville was smiling again. Everyone was happy and celebrations started in Smileville.

From that day everyone lived happily ever after.

Now the story l am going to tell is very spooky. So let's start

The woman in white

' Don't kill me Seliora ,l am your father' said Mr Huskinton

' I don't care l will kill you' said Seliora piercing the knife

' Nooooooo' shouted Mrs Peppa

Tears rolling by her chicks she sat by her son's lifeless body.Though sad but she was furious and ordered that Seliora should be put inside the room situated at the 3rd floor of their bungalow . Seliora was thrown into the room. Mrs Peppa was very sad at her order but she didn't withdraw it as her son was killed by her grandaughter. Days went by and then one day someone screamed, it was from that room where seliora was kept . Everyone rushed to the door but were afraid to go inside, they saw from the shadows that someone was killing Seliora . Mrs Peppa cried but all in vain she couldn't stop it , after sometime blood came out through the holes .Everyone was terrified and that's when Mrs Peppa ordered everyone should leave the place and go to the new bungalow . The haunted bungalow was closed and from that day no one even used the path infront of the bungalow

'These all happened in just one year,Mom' said the twenty four year aged girl Selena who was the younger sister of Seliora.

'Yes my dear, but still l remember my daughter and husband very much' said Mrs Christina Huskinton.

Selena was not happy about it because she was sure that her sister can't do such horrific thing and she doubted that there must be a mystery but she couldn't do anything because of Mrs Peppa, her grandmother.

Days went by and then one day came when Mrs Peppa announced that they would be going to the haunted bungalow for two days to do some rituals after death of Mr Huskinton which was not possible earlier because of the paranormal activities that took place.Everyone was ready and so they went there . After some cleaning it was ready to live.

Everything was going well but then a thief came and started robbing but he was seen by the security official who started chasing him. The thief ran to the third floor and saw the haunted room. He broke the magical lock which had captured the ghost and went inside. After sometime when everything was perfect he went away. The thief unknowingly bought a disaster for the Huskintons .

The next day when everyone sat down for breakfast things were very weird . Everything was flying and things were breaking. None could understand what was happening . Then a knife pierced through the priest , everything was in a chaos, then suddenly doors started to close but fortunately Selena and her mother came out. They screamed but no one could answer . Then the ghost came out and started chasing Selena. The road came to an end , Selena was very scared and was sure that she would die today. But the ghost left her and said ' Go away with your mother'. Selena couldn't understand at first but then she said ' You are my sister'.

The doors opened and Selena's mother went inside ,after sometime Selena came and she started to behave in an outrageous manner as if ghost had entered into her body. She then said ' Your plan isn't over Peppa ?'

'Selena what behaviour is this,she is your grandmother 'said Mrs Christina

'Mom , so you don't know the real identity of Peppa, then listen to me.

Seliora was very beautiful and Peppa couldn't take it so the year when l went to Seoul , she made a plan with the old priest and killed my father , then she blamed Seliora for this and killed her. Actually there is no ghost in the third floor's that room so named as haunted room.'

'Oh my god, so you told everyone but you would pay a price for that'

Saying that Peppa rushed to Mrs Christina with a knife but was blocked by Seliora

Seliora took the knife and slashed Peppa into pieces.

After that she bid goodbye to everyone and went to the heaven.

If we see this isn't that spooky but it is very beautiful.

৪০

Now the story I am going to tell is about a king who faced a very difficult situation but was able to learn a great thing.

V
KING SAKSHAMDEV

Once upon a time ruled a very proud and cruel King named Sakshamadev whose kingdom was called Sakshamrastra. It's name was Bramharastra but after Sakshamadev came to power he changed it's name . He would give people very harsh punishment at their slightest mistake.

One day he was roaming in the jungle with some of his soldiers and ministers to hunt a deer, at that time a farmer was crossing the path. When a deer came to sight , Sakshamadev was ready to shoot it just then the farmer came and seeing the farmer the deer ran away.Sakshamadev was furious and at once he ordered that the farmer should be executed. The farmer was shocked and he apologized the king a thousand times but all in vain, the king was very stubborn . The farmer was taken to the jail.

After doing such thing Sakshamadev was enjoying in the evening. He had no mercy on his people, after sometime he went to the garden and spotted something strange. It was a hole with different colours of light coming out. He put his hand inside it an was drawn into the hole.

After opening his eyes he found himself in a very different place. He started walking and went inside a house. A lady was cleaning her room with a vacuum cleaner, seeing her Sakshamadev ordered ' Hey you now go and bring water for me'

'OMG who are you and what are you doing here' saying this the lady threw her slippers on him.

Sakshamadev ran out and was flabbergasted , he saw a steel monster with four round legs and a long standing tree with no leaves but gives electric shock. He was continuously beaten up by the people of the place and it was because he didn't knew how to speak politely. The day turned into evening and then evening turned into night , Sakshamadev's stomach was mourning for food . He sat down by a cement pipe and was in low spirits when small boy came and asked 'Why are you here ?'

He replied' I don't have a place to live'

Then the boy smiled and took Sakshamadev to his house , there Sakshamadev felt very good and was happy because of the kindness shown by the boy's family. At night everyone slept, when Sakshamadev opened his eyes he was in his kingdom. He wasn't the same Sakshamadev , he had changed and now he started to help the people of his kingdom. He ordered that the farmer's execution should be stopped and after that everyone lived happily ever after.

&

This story has a lot to learn and the next story also helps in learning so let's start

VI

KIM SEON : THE ENCHANTED PRINCESS

Long long ago lived a king named Hing Zang who was a very kind , amiable and efficient ruler. He and his wife Zen Kong lived a very prosperous life but they didn't have any child and so they were very sad. They decided to call the priests to talk to god and give them a child. Everything was done , suddenly someone from the sky spoke ' You would get a boy but also a girl not '

Hing Zang was happy he got a boy but he wasn't in high spirits for his girl

The boy was named Heong Jong and the girl was named Kim Seon

Heong's childhood was great but he alsways wanted more and on the other hand Seon's childhood wasn't that great but she never complained about it . Heong was given half of the kingdom but he was never interested in that , his interests were more in gambling and wines.

When Seon turned 21 , half of the royal treasury had been finished because of Heong but without taking that in mind as a problem Hing thought that Seon was a problem and therefore she should get married.Seon didn't want to marry so soon therefore she ran away.

She walked for miles and then found a hut, she went inside and saw a boy with his dog.

He asked her ' Who are you ?'

'l am Seon'

'Oh hello, l am Kim Suhon'

'Can l live here,please'

'Ya sure'

They chatted for a while and then Seon found out that Suhon was a fighter, Seon requested him to help and told the truth, after many requests he agreed.

Seon practiced very much and then became a great fighter.

Then one day a news came that Hing was going to have a war with Chen Hong and Heong was going to help Chen Hong who had bribed him.

Seon was heartbroken and decided to help her father

She dressed up ,tied her hair and went with Suhon

They both fought and at last Hing emerged victorious

Chen and Heong were thrown behind the bars

Then Hing came and asked 'Who are you,boy'

'l am your daughter Seon, Papa'

Hing and Zen were surprised but were happy and apologized Seon for such behaviour.

Seon was the new queen and then she said' It wouldn't have been possible if Suhon wasn't there'

So Hing declared that Suhon and Seon both will rule

Seon got married to Suhon and after that everyone lived happily

'Now Stephen , tell me what you have learned today' said Grandma

'l have learned the meaning of life which is a matter of choices

I have learned that like the first story our life is full of adventures and if we want to succeed we need to fight with it

Like the second story we need to be courageous and help others in every situation which would definitely give something amazing at the last

Like the third story we think our life is horrible but actually at last we find that it is beautiful

Like the fourth story we sometimes become proud and that at the last teaches us a lesson which we should follow to succeed in life

Like the fifth story it showcases how we should respect girls who are equal to boys

' Very Good, you are correct our life is based on our choices , so do a better choice and have a wonderful life

GOODBYE !

VII
VERSE-1 MOTHER

In the garden of life, she blooms like a flower
she does her duty with strength and power.
   The one who taught me to read and write
She helped me come over my fright.
   She works day and night
For me, with anybody she can fight
   In my life, she is a boon
She is as pretty as moon
   She is as wonderful as my father
The heart of my life is my mother.

VIII
VERSE-2 FATHER

Like a shining star in the sky
A superhero who does not fly
An amazing person with fabulous personality
The one who helps me know my capability
Helps me write and read
The one acts for me as a shield
He is my sun and I am his earth
He who loves me from my birth
He is best than any other
He is none other than my Father !

IX

VERSE-3 SARS-CoV-2

Every single thing was going delicate and admirable, the integer of stories were growing and competently the number of scholar. But, the devasting and cataclysmic pathogen tumbledown everything. We lost our communication with each other and that's why every story we had, were lost. It might seem you a funny incident, but actually it was a downhearted period, as I lost more than hundred stories. After spending some days with no spirits, I again started writing stories.

Corona virus is coming
We have to do something
The virus did a roar
We have to think in our mind core
It started in China with great power
To the safe we should not take a long shower
Do not go outside in a rush
Otherwise you'll be crush

Wash hands for twenty seconds
Say it to all your friends
Don't be fright
Have a healthy diet
Corona virus has given us a task
To win it we need to wear a mask
Do not do a gathering
Feel it in your home yourself doing a cattering
The government has done a lot
With our thinking and hygiene we can win the
match with one shot.

X
LOYOLA- MY CHILDHOOD MEMORIES

'What is a school?' asked one of my friends.

A school is like a home. It not only helps a student to build a strong foundation but also helps to grow as an obedient, social and caring person. It helps in academic development and develops a person to have humanity which includes sincerity, sociality, soft-talking, obedient, caring, helpful, good behavior and determined. This helps to have a bright future' said my teacher.

I belong to Loyola school. It is situated near Fortune Tower, Xavier Square. It is a vast building with gardens, playground and a beautiful stage. The school is highly cleared and has some amazing activities.

My school is comprised of various people. Out principal, Father Victor Misquith, SJ is a fabulous man. He is amiable and has a beautiful personality. Our Vice-

Principal sister Latika is a very soft-talking women, though she is not here with us anymore as she is transferred but we miss her everyday. Our Rector Father Augustine is a sweet man. I haven't talked to him much but his behavior towards us shows that he is a great man. 'A teacher is like a candle – it consumes itself to light the way for other' is the best definition for a teacher.

All my teacher are great, Simrat Mam, Rose Minj Mam, Sridevi Mam, Jamuna Mam, Ojaswita Mam, Nilima Mam, Dawn Mam, Anju Mam, Dolon Mam, Sister Sushma, Moumita Mam, Nigel Sir, Debu Sir, Meghamala Mam,Aparna Mam, Raveleen Mam and Rikku Mam are some exceptional teachers I know. I am new to senior section but Akansha Mam, Pravakar Sir, Niharika Mam, Rashmi Mam, Hejo Mam, Haribabu Sir, Ganeshwar Sir, Vijeshree Mam, Indrani Mam, Soumya Mam, Aashima Mam, Sunita Mam, Sasmita Mam and Manasi Mam have shown that they are amazing. The other teachers whom I do not know must be fabulous and I hope to meet them.

My friends are another thing I can't leave. They help me, encourage me and stand with me even in the times of sadness. Anshuman, Asmi, Pratyaksh, Sambhavi, Shana and Koyena are some of my best friends. My partner Ankit, who sits with me, Niyati and Devanshi who sit in the next row are the ones who help me, make me laugh during the class.

My short period of life which lasts some hours in Loyola is incomplete without everyone and I hope to make them smile everyday. Thank you Loyola and thank you God for giving me such a wonderful gift: Loyola.

XI

TEACHERS-PEARLS OF WISDOM

Have we ever wondered how hard our beloved teachers work? They work at their houses and then come to help us in our studies and then again the same process is continued. We students don't go to the teacher's house to do their household work but they work hard and help us understand the concepts and in return we give them nothing except irritating them and when they scold for this, we say 'what a bad teacher', without knowing the fault is ours.

A teacher is a person who plays a pivotal role in modeling a student's life. They are the precious gems gifted by the Almighty. They are blessings from heaven. Some teachers remain in our heart for their nature. They are the ones who build a good nation and make the world a better place to live. A teacher teaches us that a pen is mightier than a sword that's why a king can only rule his kingdom but a scholar can rule the world with his knowledge.

I have heard people say that a good teacher is not hard to find but we must know where to find. I never understood this because the teachers I have come across are amiable, charming, extraordinary, energetic, composed and all great words I could use. All the teachers in my school are brilliant and other teachers also that are there in other schools. In my point of view, there is no good or bad teacher, every teacher is unique in his / her teaching style and behaviour.

The definition of a teacher is not possible because the number of good words in this world is very less. I am very grateful to have such amazing teachers in my life. We should not hut them and understand the pain they are taking for us. THANK YOU TEAHCERS !

Few Words For The Author

Shreenmay Kanungo, a good writer from LOYOLA SCHOOL, BHUBANESWAR. He is an eminent speaker. We are highly gracious to the capabilities that Shrrenmay had proven in the field of writing and poetry. He will definitely be a source of inspiration for all individual. Thank you to the entire team for their coordination and to the sucess up bringing of this book.